A note about Criollo
(cree-oh-yo)

Criollo is a difficult word to translate. The literal translation is "creole": the cultural convergence of Spanish and other European settlers in the Carribean and Latin America and their evolution throughout history.

While this definition comes close, it does not wholly evoke the same feeling that the word criollo does in me. Criollo is not only history, it is a legacy. It is in the core of who we are.

To me, Criollo refers to anything and everything that is native and unique to one's homeland. It is tied to a sentiment of pride and belonging, a feeling of familiarity and melancholy. It encompasses all national and regional cultural expressions including art, language, traditions, landmarks and food.

Immigrating to a new land is both a joyful and challenging experience. When I moved to Canada at the age of 17, I knew that there would be a world of opportunities to be discovered and that exciting times laid ahead.

As I found my way in my new home I remember a growing feeling of hunger always kept me company. Yes, hunger. As a teenage boy I was always hungry. Hungry for the flavors of the homeland that I had left behind. Hungry for my mom's home cooking and for tastes of the past. Hungry for all things Criollo.

With time, my kitchen shelf grew cluttered with cookbooks and printouts of Venezuelan cuisine; my favorite recipes were bookmarked by smudges and saucy fingerprints. Cookbooks fueled my hunger and my memories. They were a vehicle that transported me back in time to my grandmother's kitchen, where I would stare at the merengue cookies through the oven door glass and hear my 'guela complaining, "quit staring at the suspiros or they won't rise!"

This book is my little love poem to everything criollo in Venezuela. This is a collection of home and street recipes, folk tales and traditions. With this book I hope to give you a glimpse into the food and culture of my homeland: A taste of Venezuela.

On that note, many criollo foods cannot be found outside of Venezuela. This book is written for the cook abroad, so here's some acceptable substitutions for the most important criollo ingredients:

Aji Dulce: Almost everything that needs seasoning in Venezuela uses a sweet red pepper known as Aji Dulce, featured on the cover. It has a sweet, smoky flavour with a faint hint of heat as it is the only sweet pepper of the habanero family. You may find something similar in specialty markets or buy seeds online to plant your own. For this book I have used sweet bell red peppers instead.

Corn flour: This is the base of nearly everything we eat. I suggest P.A.N. yellow or white corn flour, usually found whenever Latin American products are found. However, any corn flour or finely grated pre-cooked cornmeal from the grocery store will do.

Papelon: This is an unrefined, raw and hardened sugar cane pulp used as a sweetener. When mixed with water and heat, it makes "melao" which is similar to plain molasses. All recipes in this book that call for papelon lists molasses instead.

Queso Blanco Duro: This is a salty, dry, hard cheese that is the most traditional in Venezuela. A fair substitution is Feta cheese or any unrippened aged chese.

Onoto (also called achiote or annatto): This is a small evergreen tree that grows in tropical America. Onoto seeds are used for colouring food and vegetable oils. You may find whole or ground onoto in Latin American stores or substitute with turmeric, paprika or saffron.

L. Fernando González

Tequeños

No party in Venezuela is complete without the traditional finger food "Tequeños". These deep fried cheese sticks wrapped in pastry dough are guaranteed to go fast as soon as they come out of the fryer!

The origin of Tequeños, like most criollo foods, is debated. They are likely from the city of Los Teques, where it is said a family-run catering business first started making them in the 1920s. After each event, the caterers saved the scraps of dough and cheese from pastelitos (fried cheese turnovers) and molded them into cheese sticks to serve at their own private parties.

The snacks became an instant hit and word-of-mouth made them famous across the country.

A notable fan of tequeños was former President Juan Vicente Gómez Chacó, who had them imported to the capital city of Caracas to be served at his events.

The caterers would be greeted at the Caño Amarillo train station by President Gomez's employees, who would say, "Llegaron los tequeños!" In English, this means, "The tequeños have arrived," referring to the family from Los Teques. In no time, that name was associated with the snack.

Today, tequeños remain the staple finger food at all Venezuelan parties, from birthdays to weddings.

More recently, tequeños have become a popular snack at movie theatres, with modern fillings varying from cheese to guava paste and even chocolate.

Recipe

Ingredients:

- 2 cups flour
- 5 tbsp butter, melted
- 1 egg
- 1/2 tsp salt
- 2 tbsp sugar
- 5 tbsp cold water
- 1/2 kilo hard mozarella cheese cut into sticks.
- Vegetable oil

Preparation:

Mix flour with butter, egg, salt, sugar and water. Knead into a soft dough.
Flatten dough into a rectangle and cut into strips about 1 inch wide.
Wrap strips around the blocks of cheese, sealing with a bit of water as you go around the cheese stick.
Pat all tequeños with a bit of flour to prevent them from sticking to one another.
Heat oil on a deep pot until a wooden spoon makes bubbles in it.
Fry tequeños for about 6 minutes, turning a few times so they don't burn at the bottom.
Drain and let cool for about 2 minutes on a paper towel. Serve immediately.

Tequeños can be assembled and frozen ahead of time. Fry them from frozen right before serving.

Patacones

Patacones, also called tostones, are twice-fried plantain chips served as a snack or side dish.

They are a regional dish of the Zulia estate in Venezuela, although variations of the dish appear all over Latin America. Often topped with salty cheese, ketchup or salsa rosada (ketchup and mayonnaise mixed together), they can be served as a snack or side dish to pork, grilled meats and fish.

It is thought that patacones are named after the former Argentinian currency, the patacon, because of their golden color and round shape.

Oddly, the edible patacones are not very popular in Argentina, and instead the term is often used as slang for someone who is under financial hardship. For example, you may hear someone saying, "He is so broke he doesn't even have a patacon."

You may find patacones in the chips aisle of your grocery store, but nothing beats making them from scratch!

Recipe

Ingredients:

- 1 green plantain
- Vegetable oil
- Coarse salt to taste

Preparation:

Peel and slice the plantain in one-inch thick slices.
Heat oil on medium-high until dipping a wooden spoon in it produces bubbles.
Fry the chips for about 5 minutes, turning them once.
Take them out of the fryer and placed them on a cutting board.
Flatten each chip using a spatula or meat tenderizer.
Place them back in the frying oil until they are golden and crispy.

Season with salt and serve with salty white cheese, salsa rosada or guasacaca

Guasacaca

This recipe will change your life! Before you learn how to pronounce Guasacaca, you will be putting it on everything you eat. This versatile condiment is found on nearly every table where criollo food is served.

You might say Guasacaca is the Venezuelan version of guacamole. Guasacaca, however, has many more ingredients, is more acidic and is much more heavily seasoned.

Street vendors may have a squeeze bottle filled with Guasacaca to go with anything from hamburgers to empanadas.

Guasacaca is the staple sauce to serve on parrillas (barbequed meats). It also serves as a great dip for chips and veggies.

Recipe

Ingredients:

- 1/2 red bell pepper
- 1/2 green bell pepper
- 1/2 white onion
- 1/2 tsp garlic powder
- 1/2 bunch of cilantro
- 1/8 cup vegetable oil
- 1/4 cup white vinegar, or to taste
- 1 tbsp sugar
- 2 small ripe avocados
- Salt and pepper to taste

Preparation:

Purée everything but the avocados in a blender or food processor. Once evenly combined, add avocados and purée some more.
Garnish with paprika and a twig of cilantro.
Keep refrigerated in airtight container for up to four days.

Arepas

Arepas are corn flour patties, sliced open and filled with butter and other toppings.

Arepas are the most popular meal in Venezuela. They are served daily for breakfast, lunch or dinner as a main course or as a side dish. They are an icon of national gastronomy and a beloved legacy from the Latin American aboriginal culture. Arepas bond Venezuelan people to one another across all social classes, race and ages. Everyone loves arepas!

The word arepa comes from the term "erepa", meaning "corn" in the aboriginal language of Cumanagoto. This language was spoken by the Caribe aboriginal people that lived in what is now the northeastern city of Cumaná.

Arepas are sliced open and stuffed with a variety of toppings including butter, cheese, chicken salad, pulled steak, scrambled eggs, fried pork and fish. They are sold all over the country, including arepa shops, restaurants, cafeterias, bakeries, schools, gas stations, at the beach or on the road.

Areperas (arepa shops) display assorted fillings behind glass counters, drawing patrons from the early hours before the sunrise until late at night.

Recipe

Ingredients:

- 2 cups corn flour, or as needed
- 2 cups warm water, or as needed
- 1 tsp salt
- 1 tsp vegetable oil

Preparation:

Mix water and salt together.
Slowly add corn flour while mixing with your fingers until you get a soft, smooth dough with no lumps.
Work with your hands and add more flour or water as needed: If the dough begins to crack, it means it needs more water. If it sticks to your hands and it is hard to manipulate, you may need more flour.
Cover and let stand for 5 minutes until firm.
Make balls of dough and flatten them into discs about 1/2" thick by 4" wide. Keep a bowl of water on the counter and keep your hands wet while handling the dough to keep it moist and soft.
Heat a frying pan or cast iron flat grill with a bit of oil over a moderate flame. Pre-heat oven to 400°C.
Place arepas on the grill and cook for about 10 minutes, flipping once halfway through until they have a crispy outer layer all around. It is OK if they burn a bit to black in the middle.
Once the arepas have a crispy shell, bake them in the oven for about 10-15 minutes.
Tap on the cooked arepa with your fingers, if it sounds a bit hollow it means they are ready!

To serve, slice open and fill with any of the toppings mentioned above!

Reina Pepiada

"The Beaded Queen", or La Reina Pepiada, is a chicken, avocado and green peas salad used as filling for arepas. It was created to honour Venezuela's first international beauty queen, Susana Duijm.

Susana was crowned Miss World in 1955, becoming the first Hispanic woman to win the title. Her victory also marked the beginning of Venezuelans' fascination with beauty pageants.

The story goes that an arepa vendor, filled with national pride, had his 12-year-old niece dress up as a beauty queen to pay homage to Susana. The little sovereign sat in a makeshift throne at his arepa shop. Susana's father visited the arepera and was so touched by the display he promised to come back with the beauty queen herself. He kept his promise and returned with Susana several weeks later. To mark the occasion, the vendor's mother created an arepa made especially for her. They called it La Reina Pepiada.

During that time, the word 'pepiada' (with beads) was a term of endearment for women with nice curves, such as Susana. The green peas used in the recipe gave the filling the beaded effect.

Since Susana's victory, Venezuela has accumulated more international beauty titles than any other country including five Miss World and seven Miss Universe titles.

Recipe

Ingredients:

- 2 skinless chicken breasts
- 1 avocado
- 1/2 cup mayo
- 1 tsp garlic powder
- 1 cup frozen green peas
- 2 tsp mustard
- Salt and pepper
- Lime juice

Preparation:

Place chicken breast in a saucepan with enough water to cover it.
Bring to a boil and simmer for 20 minutes or until cooked all the way through.
Drain and let cool completely.
Using your hands or two forks, pull chicken apart in strings. Set aside.
In a separate bowl, smash avocado and season with lime juice, salt and pepper.
Add mayo, mustard and garlic powder.
Mix chicken and avocado dressing together.
Cover entirely with frozen green peas and serve.

Pabellón Criollo

This ensemble of pulled steak, rice and beans is "Pabellón Criollo", the national dish of Venezuela. It is said to be inspired by the three races that make up our national heritage: Brown, White and Black.

The browned, seasoned pulled steak represents the indigenous peoples of Venezuela such as the Caribes and Yanomami. The latter is world-famous for their beautiful facial piercings and bowl-cut hair.

White rice plays the role of the Spanish conquistadors, from whom Venezuelans inherited the Spanish language.

Finally, the sweetened black beans represent African slaves who arrived with the Spanish, bringing with them a wide assortment of beliefs, music and dance that are still present today.

Together these ancesters form the Venezuelan race "mestizos", meaning mixed.

Variations of rice and beans dishes are found all around Latin America and the Caribbean. In Costa Rica and Nicaragua rice and beans are called "Gallo Pinto" (spotted rooster), in Cuba "Moros con Cristianos" (moroos and Christians), and in Panama and El Salvador "Casamiento" (marriage).

Venezuela is the only country to add carne mechada (pulled steak) to the dish, which also serves as stuffing for arepas and empanadas.

Recipe

Ingredients:

- 1 flank steak
- 1 onion, finely chopped
- 1 red pepper, diced
- 2 cloves garlic, minced
- 1 bunch parsley or cilantro
- Worcestershire sauce
- Soy sauce
- 1 tbsp Mustard
- 1/2 tsp Cumin
- Salt and pepper
- 1 cup cooked white rice
- 1 cup cooked black beans
- 2 large ripe plantains (optional)

Preparation:

Place steak on a large pot with enough water to cover it. Bring to a boil, cover and simmer for 30 minutes.
Remove steak from water. Reserve stock.
Let steak cool completely and pull apart with hands or two forks.
Sautée onion, garlic and pepper for 5 mins. Add pulled steak and stir.
Season with Worcestershire sauce, soy sauce, mustard, cumin, salt and pepper.
Add a bit of the stock and let simmer. Garnish with cilantro or parsley.
To make plantains, slice on a slight angle and fry in hot oil. Once fully cooked, place on paper towel and pat dry.

Serve steak along with rice, black beans and fried plantain.
Top the beans with a bit of sugar and a salty white cheese.

Cachapas

Cachapas are corn pancakes traditionally served with fresh Queso de Mano (a soft, milky artisan fresh cheese) and fried pork.

Like most corn dishes in Venezuela, Cachapas are a gift from our aboriginal heritage. Originally Cachapas were cooked in banana leaves and stored in clay pots, named "capachas", to take as snacks during long trips.

To this day, Cachapas are a staple roadside meal in Venezuela. They are cooked and served outdoors along busy highways.

Queso de Mano is also called "Telita", which means "fabric", because it is so soft you can peal a layer off as if you were picking up a thin piece of fabric! A good alternative is fresh mozarella cheese, the wetter the better, or fresh Oaxaca cheese.

You can try making your own Telita cheese by melting some fresh milk curd in a bit of whey, then stretching and folding the resulting mixture until you get a soft, shiny cheese. Season with salt and press with a wooden spoon against a deep dish to mold it into a disc. Flip onto a tray and refrigerate.

Recipe

Ingredients:

- 2 cups corn kernels (fresh off the corn or from a can)
- 1/2 cup corn flour
- 1 egg
- 2 tbsp sugar
- 1 tsp salt
- 1/2 cup of milk (optional)
- Vegetable oil

Preparation:

Mix all ingredients together in a blender or food processor to make a thick batter.
If needed, add milk to get the desired consistency, similar to that pancakes batter.
Let rest covered for 5 minutes. The batter will get significantly thicker.
Heat a heavy skillet over a medium flame. Rub the skillet with a little vegetable oil.
Add about 1/2 cup of the batter, spreading it out with the laddle.
If you wish to make filled cachapas, you can place a thin slice of cheese in the middle and cover it with a little more batter.
Cover and let cook for about 7 minutes or until you see bubbles on the surface.
Flip the cachapa to cook on the other side for another 5 minutes.

Serve hot with butter and a soft fresh white cheese.

Empanadas

Venezuelan Empanadas are fried corn flour patties stuffed with different fillings such as cheese, ham, beans, pulled steak, chicken or fish.

The first empanada recipe is found in the oldest recipe book known to man, written in Mesopotamia some 1700 years ago. Modern empanadas trace their origins to Galicia and Portugal, and variations are found through Southern Europe and Latin America. Spanish conquistadors brought empanadas to Venezuela in the 16th century and in no time they became a staple of local gastronomy.

Families on the north east coast of Venezuela started selling empanadas to tourists from their front porches, which made them a popular street vendor food across the country.

Front-porch empanadas are still found today. It is also very common for empanada-makers to send their children to sell at the beach or on the street. These young ambulant sellers can be heard from a mile away as they advertise their product at the top of their lungs: "Eeeeempanadas!! Eeeeeempanadas!!"

Arguably the most famous empanadas in Venezuela are found at Conejeros bazaar on Margarita Island. This busy flea market is buzzing with both locals and tourists looking to snatch a good deal and grab a bite of local fare. The empanaderas set up shop early in the morning and start the daily cook-off, each one certain that they have the best empanadas in town. Fish empanadas, made with a small shark called Cazon, is the top selling kind on the island.

Recipe

Ingredients:

- 2 cups of water
- 2 cups corn flour
- 1 tb wheat flour
- 1 tb sugar
- A pinch of salt

Vegetable oil
Any filling such as cheese, ham, pulled steak, fish, or bean.

Many of the dishes on this book can be used as a filling for empanadas.

Preparation:

Mix water, sugar and salt together and slowly add flours while mixing with your fingers.
Let rest for about 5 mins then knead again. Divide in tennis sized balls.
Place 4 cups of vegetable oil over medium high heat until a wooden spoon bubbles in it.
The oil should never smoke or else it will burn the empanadas.
Flatten a ball of dough on a piece of plastic wrap.
Make sure to wet your hands in water whenever handling the dough to prevent cracks.
Put two spoonfuls of filling in the middle of the dough and use the plastic to fold it in half, giving the empanada its iconic half-moon shape.
Seal edges by pressing down with your fingers or a fork and remove from plastic.
Slide into hot oil and fry for about 5 mins on each side or until golden brown
Place on a strainer over paper towel and let cool for five minutes before serving.

Pastel de Pescado

Pastel de Pescado (fish cake), also called Cuajao' de Pescado, is a fish and plantain casserole popular in the coastal and island cities of Venezuela.

Pastel de Pescado originated in Margarita Island, where it is called "Pastel de Chucho" and it is one of the islands most iconic dishes, made with sting ray.

Pastel de Pescado is mostly served around lent, which in Venezuela is a week long holiday called Semana Santa (holy week). Semana Santa is one of the biggest holidays in Venezuela, where children get a full week off school and families usually travel to the coastal cities for a vacation on the beach.

It is customary to give up red meats during holy week, hence the popularity of Pastel de Pescado.

The fish used is typically Cazon (shark) or chucho (sting ray), but any white fish such as Tilapia or Swordfish is acceptable. In a pinch, you could even use canned tuna!

Recipe

Ingredients:

- 6 ripe plantains
- 1.5 kilo fresh fish or 1 kilo canned fish
- 1 white onion
- 1 bunch of green onions
- 2 red peppers
- 1 bunch of leek
- 8 eggs
- 6 cloves of garlic
- 1 tbsp butter
- Vegetable oil (preferably onoto)
- Shredded cheese (optional)

Preparation:

If using fresh fish, poach for 15 mins or until cooked throughout. Let cool and flake apart.
Butter a large rectangular pan and preheat oven at 350°C.
Sautée garlic, onions, green onions, leek and peppers for about 5 mins.
Add fish and cook for another 5 minutes.
Add onoto oil for colouring, mix well and simmer for 10 mins.
Peal and slice plantains lengthwise. Fry on very hot oil until cooked throughout and set aside.
Beat the eggs until doubled in size, then fold into fish until well combined.
Layer fish and fried plantains in the pan, starting and finishing with a layer of fish.
If desired, sprinkle with cheese. Bake until golden on top. Serve immediately.

Muchacho Negro

Muchacho Negro (black boy), also called Asado Negro, is a blackened beef roast with a dark molasses gravy.

It is said the recipe came about by pure accident during colonial times in the capital city of Caracas. Many homes in Caracas had the washing sink outside, a bit of a walk from the kitchen stove, for both laundry and dishes.

This setup would lead to the unavoidable accident of leaving the roast on the stove for too long while the cook was out doing the dishes.

Housewives would be heard crying out "Ay! Se me quemó la carne!" (I burnt the roast!). To complement (or perhaps mask) this bitter burnt taste, the roast was then bathed in a sweet molasses sauce and cleverly served to guests as "Black Boy". Muchacho Negro is now a staple of home cooking across the country.

Every family has a different recipe for Muchacho Negro. Some add capers, potatoes, celery or carrots. Some use it as a filling for arepas or even as a pasta sauce.

When served on its own it is usually accompanied by fried plantains and white rice.

This is a very basic recipe for you to experiment with and add your own flavour. Just make sure to blacken the crust and sweeten the sauce, the rest is up to you.

Recipe

Ingredients:

- 1 inside round eye beef roast
- 1/2 cup vegetable oil
- 3 tbsp molasses
- 1 large onion, chopped
- 5 cloves of garlic, chopped
- 2 cups red wine
- 1 cup beef stock
- Salt and pepper

Preparation:

Rub roast with garlic, salt and pepper.
Heat oil on medium-high and brown roast for about 15 minutes, until completely blackened.
Remove from pan and set aside.
Add onion and cook until translucent.
Add wine and beef stock.
Cook on medium-low until the liquid is reduced by half, about 20mins.
Place the roast back in the pan and cover with sauce.
Bake at 300°C for about 2 hours.
Let rest for about 5 minutes. Slice and serve.

Bollos Pelones

Bollos Pelones (bald tamales) are corn flour patties filled with ground beef and topped with tomato sauce.

They get their name from the fact that they are not wrapped in banana or corn leaves like most tamales. Instead, they are dropped directly in boiling water, which gives them their shiny bald look.

Bollos, as well as Hallacas, are the Venezuelan version of tamales, popular across all Latin America. Bollos take many shapes and names depending on their ingredients and preparation.

Bollos Pelones are said to come originally from Yaracuy state, where they are traditionally made with pork instead of beef. Some coastal cities fill them with fish.

Mostly a home cooked dish, in the mid 1900s Bollos were known to be middle class fare. Nowadays bollos are found in most households across the country.

You can substitute the filling for ground pork or fish, or serve them plain with your eggs at breakfast!

Recipe

Ingredients:

Dough
- 2 ½ cups corn flour, or as needed
- 2 cups lukewarm water, or as needed
- 1 tsp salt

Fillings
- 2 lb ground beef or pork
- 1 tsp olive oil
- 1 large onion, finely chopped
- 4 cloves garlic, chopped
- 1 red pepper, finely chopped
- 1 tbsp beef stock concentrate
- Salt, pepper and hot sauce

Toppings
- 1 tsp olive oil
- 1 onion, finnely chopped
- 5 cloves of garlic, chopped
- 1 can of crushed tomatoes
- 1 red pepper, finely chopped
- 2 cups red wine
- Salt, pepper, oregano to taste
- Parmesan cheese

Preparation:

Mix water and salt and slowly add flour while mixing with your hands to form a soft dough with no lumps.
Cover dough and let stand for 5 minutes until firm.
Sautée garlic, onion and pepper in olive oil until cooked. Add ground meat and stir.
Add beef stock concentrate for added flavor. Season with salt, pepper and hot sauce to taste.
Cook until liquid has evaporated and meat has browned. Set aside.
For tomato topping, sautée onions, garlic and red pepper in olive oil until cooked.
Add tomatoes and wine. Season with salt, pepper and oregano.
Cook on low heat until liquid has evaporated by half.
Dive dough in tennis sized balls. Dip your thumb in the middle of each to make a cavity.
Fill it with 2 tbsp of ground beef and seal, using with a bit of water.
Work the bollo into the desired shape, usually a ball or egg shaped.
Bring a large pot of salted water to a gentle boil and cook the bollos for about 10 minutes.
Drain and let cool for about 5 minutes. Top with butter, tomato sauce and parmesan cheese

Hallacas

"Huele a Navidad!", criollo words for "Christmas is in the air". You will hear them uttered when the scent of banana leaves and guiso fill the air in Venezuelan kitchens. It means Hallacas are cooking in the stock pot.

Hallacas are corn flour patties filled with stewed beef, chicken, pork, capers, olives and raisins, wrapped in banana leaves and traditionally served with chicken salad and ham bread over Christmas time.

The making of hallacas marks the start of the holiday season. Family members and friends come together while traditional drinks (Ponche Crema) and music (Gaitas) contribute to the festive atmostphere.

Known to be very labor intensive, hallacas are made in large batches over several days. Scenes of mothers scolding children for stealing bits of fillings and men complaining of being left to clean leaves or to do last minute shopping are all part of the fun of this dearly beloved tradition.

It is customary for families and friends to exchange hallacas and to offer them to all visitors over the month of December. Friendly rivalry over whose hallacas are the best is part of the holiday culture, and you can often hear the popular expression, "La mejor hallaca la hace mi mamá" throughout the month. "The best hallaca is the one my mother makes."

This is my mamá Nilza's hallaca recipe, which really is the best :)

Recipe

Ingredients:

Guiso (filling)
- 1.5 lbs pork roast, diced
- 3 lbs beef roast, diced
- 3 lbs chicken thighs, diced
- 1 lb bacon, finely chopped
- 1 lb onion, finely chopped
- ½ cup garlic, minced
- 1 lb leek
- ½ lb green onion
- 1.5 lbs red pepper
- 2 cups red wine
- 1 cup molasses
- 1/2 cup capers
- 1 cup raisins, soaked in red wine
- Mustard, Salt, Pepper, Cumin and Workshire sauce and hot sauce to taste

Dough
- 3 packs of corn flour
- 3 cups chicken stock
- 1 cup oil with onoto (also known as annato or achiote)

Toppings and Assembly
- 1 lb bell peppers, julienned
- 1 lb white onion, cut into rings
- 1 cup pepper-filled olives
- 1 cup raisins
- 1 lb boneless chicken
- Vegetable oil with onoto
- 6 packs banana leaves
- White cooking string

Preparation:

To make the dough, mix in batches chicken stock, molasses and oil. Slowly add flour and work into a soft dough.
For the filling, season diced meats with mustard, salt, pepper, cumin, workshire sauce and red wine to taste.
Sautée bacon and add onions, garlic, leek, green onions and red pepper.
Add meats and hot sauce to taste. Add red wine and molasses and let simmer until meat is tender. Let cool
For the toppings, poach chicken for 20 mins and let cool. Pull apart into strings and set aside.
Wash banana leaves, cut the stems out and divide in 15-inch wide rectangles.
Form a fistful of dough into a ball and dip in coloured vegetable oil. Flatten ball on a single banana leaf.
Add a scoop of stew, 2 pepper slices, 1 white onion ring, 1 olive, 2 raisins, a few chicken strings.
Fold into a rectangle and wrap with a second leaf. Tie with white cooking string. Repeat with all dough and stew.
Cook in boiling water for 50 mins from frozen or 30 mins from thawed. Serve on a single banana leaf.

Cachitos y Pan de Jamón

Cachitos, meaning little horns, are crescent rolls filled with ham and bacon. They are one of the most popular breakfast food in Venezuela, along with arepas, and are sold fresh off the oven at bakeries and cafeterias.

Cachitos are typically accompanied by freshly-squeezed orange juice or coffee for a quick on-the-go breakfast. You could say they are the criollo version of the French croissant.

The same dough can be used for Pan de Jamón (ham bread), which is made mostly around Christmas time.

Pan de Jamón is essentially a larger version of the Cachito, filled with ham, bacon, olives and raisins to complement other Christmas meals, such as Hallacas.

Unlike most Venezuelan recipes, these are not usually home made. They are two staples of Venezuelan bakeries.

The beloved panaderías, or bakeries, are where Venezuelans go for bread, coffee, breakfast and lunch, as well as other convenience shopping. They can be found on practically every corner.

Due to the steep competition, panaderias are usually very secretive about their recipes. So keep this one under lock and key, because it is truly a gem :)

Recipe

Ingredients:

Dough
- 1 stick of butter, melted
- 1 egg
- 1 cup milk
- 4 cups flour
- 1/2 cup sugar
- 1 tbsp instant granulated yeast

Fillings for Chachito:
- 200 grams black forest ham, julliened
- 1/2 lb of bacon, finely chopped
- 1 egg
- 1 tsp molasses

Fillings for Pan de Jamón:
- 200 grams black forest ham, sliced
- 1/2 lb of bacon
- 1/2 cup pepper filled olives
- 1/2 cup raisins
- 1 egg
- 1 tsp molasses

Preparation:

If you have a bread-maker, just dump all the ingredients (wet first, dry last) and start the cycle of dough.
If using electric mixer, fill the bowl with the dry ingredients. Use the dough hook and slowly add the wet ingredients.
Once combined, knead by hand until you get an uniform dough.
Cover and let rise for 1 hour on a warm spot.
Preheat oven at 350°C. Whisk egg and molasses into an egg wash.
Divide dough in three balls. Flatten each ball into rectangles using a rolling pin.
Wet the edges of the dough with egg wash using a brush.
If making cachitos, cut each rectangle in about 10-12 triangles. Distribute ham and bacon evenly across all triangles. To form each cachito, fold in two corners and roll into the third corner in a crescent shape.
If making pan de jamón, add fillings evenly across the three rectangles.
Fold in the ends and roll up into a cylinder. Poke holes with a fork on the top.
Brush with egg wash and bake for about 40mins or until golden brown. Let cool for 10 minutes before serving

Pisca Andina

Pisca Andina is a creamy potoato and cilantro soup. It is traditionally served for breakfast, topped with a poached egg and smoked cheese.

Did you party a bit much last night? The soothing, warm embrace of "Pisca Andina" is a favourite Venezuelan secret to nurse the unwanted "Ratón" (hangover). Pisca is a miraculous, delicious gift from the Venezuelan Andes.

Venezuela is home to a wide diversity of landscapes. Vibrant cities all across the country contrast tropical beaches, the Amazonas rainforest and a sand dune dessert which unexpectedly neighbours the beautiful snowy Andes.

People from the Venezuelan Andes - friendly nicknamed "Gochos" - are known for their hospitality, gentle manners and colorful small towns filled with artisan shops.

Warm soups are quite popular around the Andes due to their cold temperatures year round.

It is said Pisca Andina is the way Gochos get the body warmed up before the day's start.

Recipe

Ingredients:

- 5 Large potatoes, peeled and diced
- 1 lt chicken broth
- 4 cloves of garlic, chopped
- 1 bunch of green onion, finely chopped
- 1 bunch fresh cilantro, finely chopped
- 1/4 kg of smoked cheese, diced (eg, smoked cheddar)
- 1/2 lt whole milk
- 1 tbsp butter
- 4 eggs
- Salt, pepper and hot sauce to taste

Preparation:

Heat up butter in a large stock pot over medium heat
Sautée garlic and green onions for about 5 minutes
Add chicken stock and potatoes
Cook until the potatoes are soft
Add milk, salt and pepper
Cook for about 10 mins, stirring occasionally
Break one egg into a cup and gently drop into the broth. Repeat with all four eggs.
Add cilantro and cheese, and reduce heat to a simmer.
Cook until the eggs are poached and remove from heat

Serve in clay bowls with arepas and hot sauce to taste

Buñuelos de Yuca

Buñuelos de Yuca are sweet fritters made of cassava drizzled with molasses, honey or dulce de leche.

Buñuelos have traveled a long way from the Moorish, to the Spanish and across all Latin America. Originally made with flour and sugar, similar to a donut hole, Buñuelos have been reinvented from country to country using many ingredients such as banana plantains, cheese and corn. In Venezuela, Buñuelos de Yuca are the most traditional.

Yuca, or cassava, is the one of worlds most cultivated starches and a major staple food in the developing world, providing a basic diet for more than five hundred million people.

In Venezuela, Yuca is usually boiled then grilled or fried and served as a side dish for barbequed meats. It is also the main ingredients in Casabe, a crunchy flatbread inherited from the Venezuelan aboriginal culture and served with practically every meal.

In the 1700s acclaimed benedictine monk and historian Inigo Abbad wrote a travel journal entitled Voyage to America, published in Caracas two centuries later. In this diary Abbad recounted his trips to Cumana, Margarita island, New Barcelona and the Orinoco river. He declared Buñuelos de Yuca as the traditional gift during Easter and Christmas. Few follow this tradition today, instead Bunuelos are made sporadically throughout the year as a snack or dessert.

Recipe

Ingredients:

- 2 lbs of yuca or cassava
- 3 egg yolks, beaten
- 1/4 cup granulated sugar
- 1/3 tsp salt
- Vegetable oil
- Molasses, honey or Dulce de Leche
- Powder sugar

Preparation:

Peal and cut the yuca
Cook on boiling water until soft, about 30 minutes.
Drain and let cool.
Remove the inner stem of each yuca root
Mash using hands or potato masher.
Add salt, sugar and egg yolks.
Kneed into an uniform dough.
Divide into golf sized balls and set aside.
Heat a large pot of vegetable oil on medium-high.
Deep fry buñuelos until golden, about 6 minutes.
Remove from oil and place on paper towel.
Drizzle with Molasses, honey or dulce de leche and sprinkle with powder sugar.

Bonus recipe! Make your own Dulce de Leche:

Remove the label from a can of condensed milk and open two holes on the top of it.

Place the can in a large pot and fill with water one inch from the top of the can. To avoid rattling you can place a cloth under the can.

Bring the water to a boil then lower the heat to medium and let cook for 3 hours. If the water evaporates, add some more part way through.

Carefully remove the can from the boiling water and let cool. When you open it you'll have dulce de leche in a can!

Tres Leches

Torta tres leches (three milks cake) is a sponge cake soaked in a creamy sauce, topped with meringue and garnished with cinnamon.

Its origins are disputed among Latin American and European countries. The Italians say it's a variation of tiramisu and the British claim it is a lovechild of the rum cake and trifle.

Tres leches first made its way into kitchens across Latin America in 1950 in the form of a recipe printed on the back of Nestle canned milks.

This cake is surprisingly easy to make and can stay refrigerated for several days. It is perfectly acceptable to use white cake mix for this recipe instead of making it from scratch.

Recipe

Ingredients:

Cake
- 1 1/2 cups cake flour, sifted
- 1/2 tablespoon baking powder
- Pinch of salt
- 1 stick butter, room temperature
- 3/4 cup sugar
- 3 eggs
- 3/4 cup milk

Milk sauce
- 1 can (12 oz) evaporated milk
- 1 can (14 oz) condensed milk
- 2 cans (6 oz eachl) thick cream

Topping
- 3 egg whites
- 1/2 cup sugar
- 1/8 tsp white vinegar
- Cinnamon

Preparation:

Mix all dry ingredients together and set aside.
Cream butter and sugar until fluffy. Add eggs one at a time and mix until combined.
Continue mixing on low speed and alternate between milk and dry ingredients.
Mix all for another 30 seconds at 350°C. Pour into oiled and floured 8-inch cake pan.
Bake 30-40 minutes or until a knife inserted into center comes out clean; let cool completely.
For the milk sauce, whisk all of the milks together.
Take the cooled cake out of the pan and slice in half horizontally.
Put the bottom half back in the pan and, using a ladle, soak the cake with 1/3 of the milk mixture.
Place the top half back on upside down, so that the spongy side is facing up.
Pour the rest of the milk sauce evenly across the entire cake.
For the topping, beat egg whites until white and fluffy. Add sugar and beat for another minute to form stiff peaks.
Sprinkle vinegar and beat for another 15 seconds.
Spread the meringue onto the cake and make peaks using a fork or piping bag.
Place under broiler for about 2 minutes or until peaks are hard and gold. Let cool.
Sprinkle with cinnamon and refrigerate overnight.

Quesillo

Quesillo, meaning little cheese, is a custard dessert with burnt caramel topping. It is similar to caramel flan, which is found throughout Latin America.

The difference between flan and quesillo is that the latter uses whole eggs instead of just egg whites. This creates small air bubbles in the custard, making it look like traditional Venezuelan white cheese. Despite the name of the dessert, there isn't actually any cheese in quesillo.

Quesillo is regularly part of the traditional birthday trio, served at parties alongside cake and Jell-o. It can also be served at Christmas, adorned with raisins and nuts. On Margarita Island, the milk is sometimes substituted with coconut milk and the quesillo is topped with shredded coconut.

Quesillo is traditionally cooked in a special quesillo or flan container. This is a deep baking tin with an airtight lid.

If you do not have a quesillo tin, you may use any 8" round, 6" deep pie plate or casserole dish with a lid or wrapped in tin foil.

Recipe

Ingredients:

- 4 eggs
- 1 can (14oz) condensed milk
- 1 can (14ox) evaporated milk
- 1 cup milk
- 1 tbsp vanilla
- 1 tbsp dark rum
- 1 cup sugar

Preparation:

Place sugar with a bit of water on a frying pan.
Cook over a medium low flame until sugar turns into dark amber caramel syrup.
Take caramel off the heat and pour on quesillo tin or pie plate.
Swirl around until caramel hardens and evenly coats the walls and bottom of the tin.
Combine all other ingredients in a blender for 5 minutes.
Pour over hardened syrup. Cover tin and place in large baking pan.
Pour boiling water on the baking pan and around the tin to create a double boiler
Bake at 350°C for about 35 minutes or until a knife inserted in the middle comes out clean.
Let cool and refrigerate for at least 2 hours or until fully set.
Run a butter knife around the edge of the quesillo to release it from the tin.
Gently flip over a platter and serve.

Golfeados

They're Criollo, they're sticky and they're delicious! Golfeados are Venezuelan sticky buns with an unexpected combination of raw brown sugar, salty cheese and sweet anise seeds.

Golfeados originated in the capital region of Venezuela, likely from the neighbourhood of Petare around the 1950s.

It was during this time that thousands of European families immigrated to Venezuela. Italians and Portuguese immigrants were quickest to set up shop, opening bakeries - called Panaderias - all around the country.

The high volume of bakeshops created a creative war among bakers, resulting in a large variety of breads and baked goods. Golfeados are one delicious result of this competition.

They may take their inspiration from the French snail pastry or the North American cinnamon roll, but Golfeados are as Criollo as it gets!

This recipe is traditionally made with panela or papelon, which you can find at any store that sells Latin American products. It is usually sold solid, and you can ground it in the food processor. If you cannot find panela, use light brown sugar seasoned with a bit of nutmeg.

Similarly, the cheese is usually Queso Blanco, but you can use any salty white including Queso Anejo, Halloom, Feta or even Pecorino.

Recipe

Ingredients:

Dough
- 1 stick of butter, melted
- 1 egg
- 1 cup milk
- 4 cups flour
- 1/2 cup sugar
- 1 tbsp. instant granulated yeast
- 1/2 tbsp. anise or fennel seeds

Fillings and Toppings
- 1 cup molasses
- 1 cup finely ground panela
- 1 cup white salty cheese
- 1/2 tbsp. anise or fennel seeds
- 1 cup shredded mozzarella cheese

Preparation:

If you have a bread-maker, just dump all the ingredients (wet first, dry last) and start the cycle of dough.
If using electric mixer, fill the bowl with the dry ingredients. Use the dough hook and slowly add the wet ingredients.
Once combined, knead by hand until you get an uniform dough.
Cover and let rise for 1 hour on a warm spot.
Flatten dough into a large rectangle about 1/2 inch thick. Spread 1/2 cup molasses using a pastry brush.
Sprinkle panela, salty cheese and anise seeds. Tightly roll from the widest side to form a log.
Cut with a knife into rolls, about 3 inches wide. Place on a deep baking tray, cover and let rise again for 20 mins.
Preheat oven to 350°C. Mix remaining molasses with 1/2 cup warm water.
Brush over rolls and set remaining molasses wash aside.
Bake rolls for 10 minutes. Remove from oven and brush again.
Bake for another 5 minutes. Remove and brush again. Bake for another 5 minutes or until fully cooked.
Once they are done, use a spatula to place them on a non-stick cookie sheet or parchment paper.
Let rest for 5 minutes, top with mozzarella cheese and serve warm.

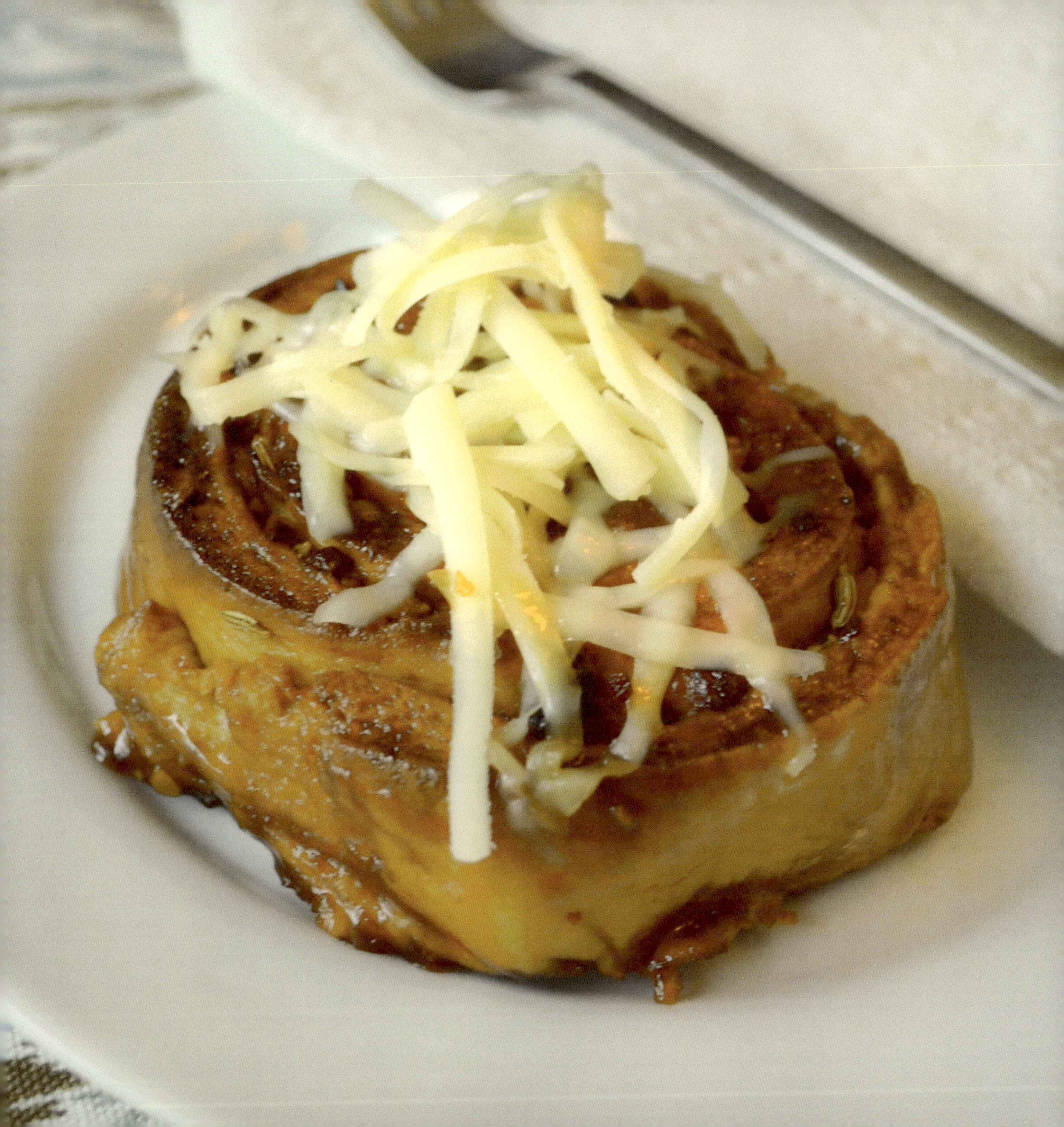

Pie de Parchita

This sweet and tart dessert is offered in restaurants and at bakeries throughout Venezuela.

The recipes vary widely and span from a traditional French mousse, to a creamy cheesecake, or a combination of the two.

Passion fruit takes many names across Latin America including maracuyá, parcha or chinola. In Venezuela, it is called Parchita. Venezuela is the 5th producer of passion fruit in the world, though neighboring countries such as Brazil and Colombia make up about 90% of the worldwide production.

Parchitas are mostly consumed in juices, ice creams and desserts.

When shopping for fresh passion fruit look for a yellow or purple skin, hard to the touch and with lots of wrinkles and dimples. If you cannot find fresh fruit, you can substitute for frozen pulp.

Recipe

Ingredients:

The crust
- 1/4 cup butter
- 1/4 cup sugar
- 1 egg
- 1 cup flour
- 1/8 tsp. salt
- 1/4 cup cold water

The filling
- 1/2 cup passion fruit pulp (about 10 passion fruits)
- 250 grams cream cheese
- 1/4 cup sugar
- 1 can evaporated milk
- 1 envelope flavourless gelatin
- 1 cup hot water

The topping
- 1/4 cup passion fruit pulp (about 5 passion fruits)
- 1/2 cup sugar
- 1 envelope flavourless gelatin
- 1 cup hot water

Preparation:

Cream butter and sugar together using an electric mixer. Add egg and mix until just combined.
Whisk together flour and salt and add to mixture all at once. Add water slowly.
Lightly flour and oil a tart pan with removable bottom or a spring form pan.
Press the dough against the bottom and sides of the pan. Poke vents in the crust with a fork.
Refrigerate for 15 mins. Preheat oven to 400 degrees and bake crust for 15 mins or until golden. Let cool.
For the filling, puree pulp in blender and press through strainer to remove the seeds.
Beat cream cheese and sugar using an electric mixer until smooth. Add pulp and evaporated milk.
Dissolve gelatin in water and slowly add to batter until fully combined.
Pour over crust and refrigerate until set, at least 2 hours.
For the topping, dissolve gelatin and sugar in hot water. Add pulp, including seeds.
Place bowl in an ice bath to cool mixture to room temperature. Gently ladle the topping onto the mousse.
Refrigerate until set, about 30 minutes.
Carefully pop out of pan and serve cold.

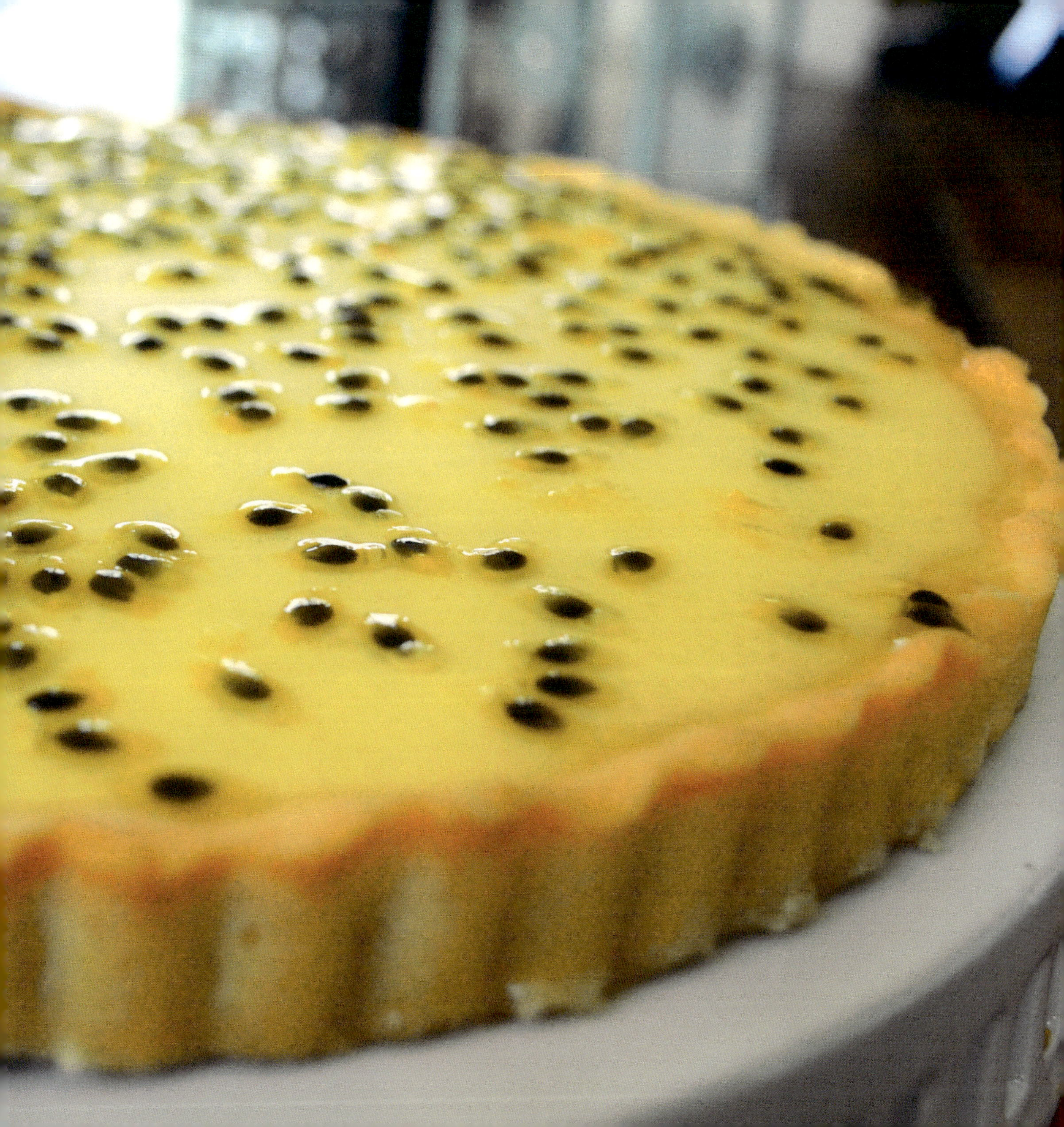

Dulce de Lechosa

Dulce de Lechosa, or candied papaya, is a spiced green papaya preserve.

This dessert is most popular around the December holiday season; however, Dulce de Lechosa can be enjoyed throughout the year on its own, on a cracker or with a slice of cream cheese.

Dulce de Lechosa is usually given as a present on its own or in a gift basket.

Like most preserves in Venezuela, they are most often sold on the side of the road in sealed glass jars.

The greener the papaya, the more translucent your slices will become after cooking.

This is a very basic recipe but you can make it your own by adding other ingredients to the preserve such as figs, cinnamon or raisins.

Recipe

Ingredients:

- 1 large green papaya (about 2lbs)
- 2 tsp baking soda
- 6 cups sugar
- 1/4 cup molasses
- Whole cloves

Preparation:

Cut papayas lengthwise and remove seeds. Use a peeler to remove skin and slice in one inch thick slices.
Fill a large pot with water and add baking soda. Add papaya and let rest for one hour. Drain and set aside.
Bring 4 liters of water to a boil. Add whole cloves and sugar.
Add papaya and lower heat to a medium-low.
Cook for 2 to three hours or until the water becomes a smooth caramel sauce.
Add molasses and stir.

Let rest overnight or store in sealed sterilized jars for up to a year.

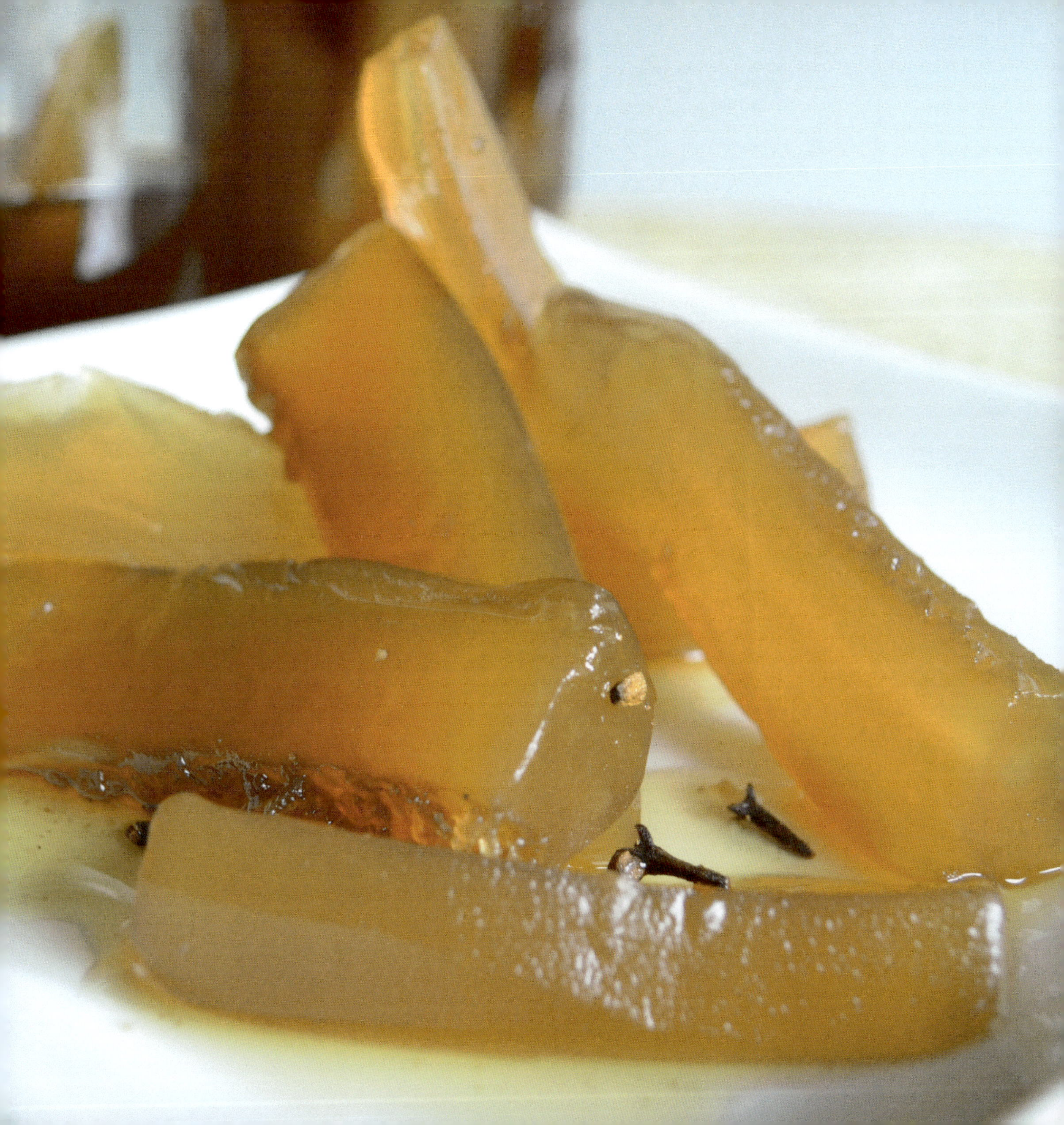

Chicha

In Venezuela, chicha criolla is a creamy drink made with rice, served on ice and topped with cinnamon.

Chicha is a gift from our aboriginal ancestors, originally made of fermented corn as an alcoholic drink.

Many variations appear all across South America and they include ingredients such as maize, yucca, quinoa or potatoes. In the Venezuelan state of Tachira, chicha andina is made with fermented pineapple.

The wide variation of chicha, from a bitter alcoholic cocktail to a sweet creamy drink, led to the popular saying, "Eso no es chicha ni limonada" meaning, "That's neither chicha nor lemonade". This is used to describe things that are neither here or there, thus hard to place in a specific category.

Chicha criolla (also called chicha de arroz, or rice chicha) is most popular across Venezuela. It is refreshing, creamy and sweet. Since it is non-alcoholic, chicha criolla is most popular among young children, who usually like to top it with condensed milk.

Chicha is typically sold by street vendors out of mobile carts. These vendors are called chicheros and are a staple of Venezuelan street cuisine.

You will usually find a chichero around the corner from a school or near a busy street mall, wearing a white robe and pouring the rice milkshake onto disposable cups using a giant ladle.

Recipe

Ingredients:

- 1 cup white rice
- 1 cup whole milk
- 1 cup condensed milk
- 1 cup evaporated milk
- 1/2 tsp vanilla extract
- 6 tbsp sugar
- 1 cinnamon stick
- 1 dash of salt

Preparation:

Soak the rice in two cups of water overnight.
Rinse and place in a deep pot with cinnamon stick and seven cups of water.
Cook over medium heat for 35 minutes. Remove from heat and let cool.
Working in batches with a blender, purée rice with all milks, sugar, salt and vanilla.
Refrigerate in airtight container for at least an hour.

Serve over crushed ice and top with ground cinnamon and condensed milk.

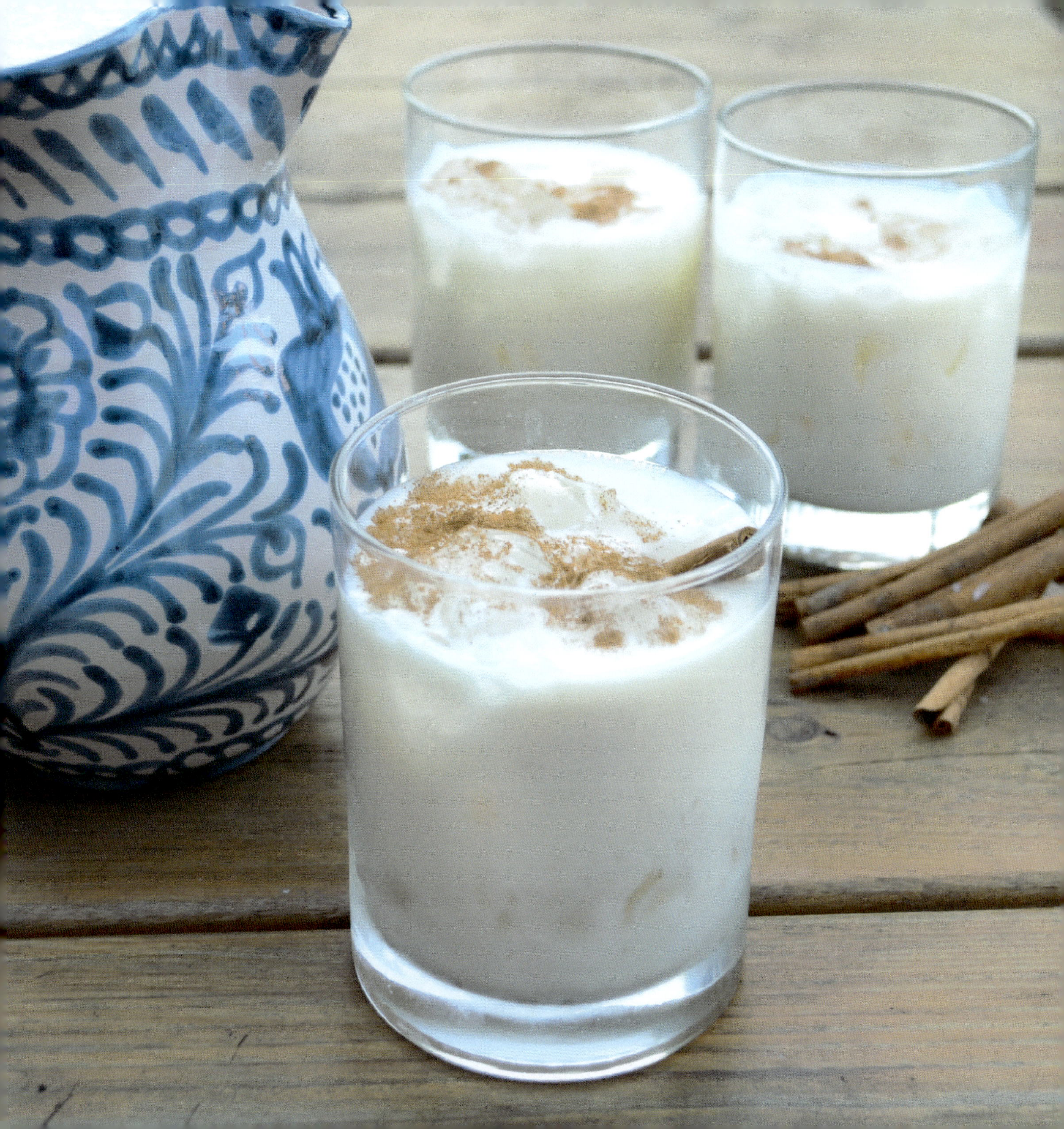

Dedicado a mi 'guela
Maria Chacin de Manzano

Special thanks to all my friends and family
for their contributions and support on the making of his book

Printed in Poland
by Amazon Fulfillment
Poland Sp. z o.o., Wrocław